America's Neighborhoods

America's Neighborhoods

Bonnie B. Armbruster

Charles L. Mitsakos

Vincent R. Rogers

Ginn and Company

Bonnie B. Armbruster is currently Assistant Professor at the Center for the Study of Reading at the University of Illinois, where she conducts research on reading and on studying in the content areas. Dr. Armbruster has published numerous articles on content-area reading in social studies and in other disciplines.

Charles L. Mitsakos is Superintendent of Schools in Winchester, Massachusetts. A former elementary school teacher and social studies supervisor, he is also a lecturer in curriculum and instruction. Dr. Mitsakos is the author of a variety of social studies materials and has served as a consultant to schools throughout the United States.

Vincent R. Rogers is a Professor of Education with an emphasis on social studies education at the University of Conneticut. A former Fulbright Scholar at the University of London and author of *Social Studies in British Education,* Dr. Rogers has written extensively about social studies education in *Social Education, Learning, The Instructor, Phi Delta Kappan,* and *Educational Leadership.*

Credits appear on page 160.

TABLE OF CONTENTS

Unit 1 What Is a Neighborhood?

8

Unit 2 Neighbors Have Needs

36

Maps, Charts, and Graphs

Unit 1 What is a Neighborhood?

I said good-bye
   to the old neighborhood
Said I'd like to take you with me
   if I could
Said good-bye to my friends
   and the old oak tree
And they all said good-bye to me.

Words You Will Use

state	neighborhood
weather	neighbor
past	ocean

The Big Question

How are neighborhoods alike?
How are they different?

Skills in This Unit

Interpreting Visual Data

Lesson 1

Dad's Surprise

"Your dad has a surprise for you," said Mom.

"Oh boy!" said Ben. "I love surprises."

"Why don't you guess what it is?" asked Dad.

"Oh no! Not that again!" cried Sarah.

"You always ask us to guess. Just tell us!"

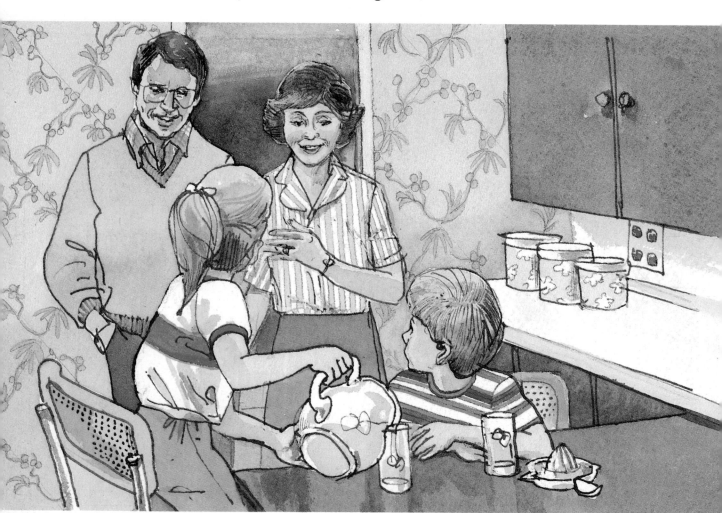

"Well, okay," said Dad. "We're moving."

"That's not funny, Dad," said Sarah.

"I'm not joking," said Dad quietly, "I have a new job. It's a better one. The work is more interesting. The job will give us more money to buy the things we need."

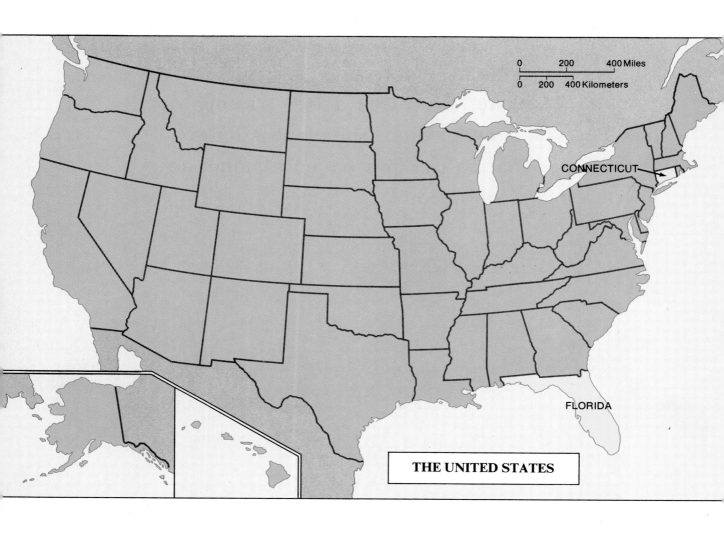

THE UNITED STATES

"Maybe we could still live here," Ben said.
"Dad, can't you take a train to your new job?"

"No, my job is too far away," said Dad.

"It's in the **state** of Florida," said Mom.

"Florida," cried Ben. "Where's Florida?"

"About a million miles away from Connecticut," answered Sarah.

"It's not that far," smiled Dad. "But it is far."

"Florida is different from Connecticut. It's hot all the time," said Sarah.

"It is very different," said Mom. "It's so warm you can swim almost every day of the year."

Ben's eyes got big. Swimming!

Lesson 1 Review

1. Why are Ben and Sarah moving?
2. How do you think they feel about moving?
3. Tell about the weather where you live.

Lesson 2

We Live in a Neighborhood

"I don't want to leave this town," said Ben. "It's a nice **neighborhood.**"

"A town isn't a neighborhood, Ben," said Sarah. A neighborhood is just part of a town. Our neighborhood is the part of town closest to us."

"Part of our neighborhood is this street,"
Sarah went on. "Another part is all the streets
and houses between here and the school. But I
guess the best part is the people."

Ben was still unhappy.

"I won't know the streets in the new neighborhood," said Ben. "And we won't have any friends there."

"Maybe we can make some new friends," said Sarah. But she wasn't really sure. Ben could tell that she was just trying to cheer him up.

Lesson 2 Review

1. What things are in a neighborhood?
2. Why are Ben and Sarah unhappy about moving?

Lesson 3

Two Neighborhoods

It isn't easy saying good-bye to old friends. Sarah and Ben will miss their old neighborhood. They will miss the snowy winter **weather.** They will miss the familiar houses. Most of all, they will miss their friends.

Sarah and Ben's new neighborhood seems different and strange to them. They will have to learn where everything is. They will have to get used to the warm winter weather. Hardest of all, they will have to make new friends.

Not everything will be different for Ben and
Sarah. Some things in their old neighborhood
are in their new neighborhood, too. Can you think
what some of these things are?

Every neighborhood has people. Soon Sarah and Ben will meet their new neighbors.

Lesson 3 Review

1. Look at the two neighborhoods on pages 18 and 19. What is different about them?
2. Use the pictures on pages 20 and 21 to find ways that the two neighborhoods are alike.
3. Do you think Ben and Sarah will be happy in their new neighborhood? Why or why not?

Lesson 4

New Neighbors

"Welcome to the neighborhood," said a man who came to the door. "We thought you might like something to eat," said his wife.

"That is kind of you," said Mom. "Please come in."

These people are **neighbors.** Neighbors live in the houses or apartments closest to you.

"It looks like you could use some help, neighbor," said another man from the next yard.

"Thanks!" said Dad. "We just moved from Connecticut."

"Welcome!" said the neighbor. "We live next door. Our children are happy to see your family moving in."

"Do you think those kids will play with us?"
Ben asked.

"Let's ask," said Sarah. "Maybe we can play
catch."

"What if they say no?" Ben said.

"Oh, Ben!" Sarah said. "They could be our
new friends."

"I'm Sarah and this is Ben."

"I'm Joyce."

"I'm Kevin. Want to play catch?"

"Sure!" said Sarah. "See, Ben, we can make new friends."

Lesson 4 Review

1. Why did the neighbor come to visit?

2. How can neighbors help each other?

3. What can the children do?

Special Feature

Celebrations: Having Fun Together

Neighbors get together at special times to celebrate. Some celebrations help us remember the **past.** They remind us of what our country was like long ago. This is a Fourth of July parade. People are celebrating the birthday of the United States.

Some celebrations are just for fun.
People get together in large and small groups
to celebrate happy events or things from
the past. When celebrating, everyone feels
part of one big family.

A Walk Around

"You will like our neighborhood," said Joyce. "It's a friendly place to live."

"This is Mangrove Mall," said Kevin. "There are lots of stores with everything you could want."

"Let's go in this store," said Sarah.

"No stopping!" said Ben. "We're on a walk!"

"This is where we go to school," said Joyce. "Maybe we can walk to school together."

"Hey, Kevin, let's see if those guys will play ball with us," yelled Ben.

"No stopping," reminded Sarah. "Remember, we're on a walk."

"The **ocean** is just a little further down
this street," explained Joyce.

"We lived near an ocean in our old
neighborhood, too," said Ben.

"It's the same ocean," said Sarah.

"Let's go see it!" cried Joyce.

"This is the best part of the walk," said Kevin.

"You're right!" said Ben.

"This is nice, just as Connecticut was," said Sarah.

Lesson 5 Review

1. What did the children see on their walk?

2. What things would you see on a short walk around your neighborhood?

Skills for Thinking

The New Neighborhood

A map is a picture of a place. This is a map of Sarah's and Ben's new neighborhood.

1. Find Sarah's and Ben's house.
2. Who lives next door?
3. What is the name of their street?

Look at the map again. Read the story.

Sarah was sick. Ben had to walk to school alone. He came to the corner of Beach Street and Coral Road.

1. Which way should Ben turn to go to school?
2. On which street would Ben find the police station?
3. Which way should Ben turn to mail a letter?

Unit **1** Review

Summary

- A neighborhood is a place where people live near one another.
- Every neighborhood is special.

The Big Question

**How are neighborhoods alike?
How are they different?**

Using Your New Words

Match each word to a picture.

ocean   state   neighborhood   neighbor

Test

Testing Skills

1. Think about someone moving into your neighborhood. What places would you want to show them? Draw a picture of some of these places.

2. Follow the trip Ben and Sarah made from Connecticut to Florida. How many states did they go through?

Unit 2 Neighbors Have Needs

Here is part of another neighborhood. It is different from Sarah's and Ben's. What differences can you see? The people in both neighborhoods have needs. Some of their needs are the same.

Words You Will Use

communicating   need
want   product
service   electricity

The Big Question

How do people get what they need?

Skills in This Unit

Organizing Information

Lesson 1

Messages

"There are a lot of messages here," said Julie. "Do you think anyone will see our sign?"

"Of course," said her brother, Tom. "Everybody stops to read them. Put it up right there."

"Maybe we should have made it bigger," said Julie. "I hope somebody finds Toby soon."

"I see somebody lost a cat," said Mr. Vargas.

"Oh, yes," said Julie. "We just have to get him back."

"You could put an ad in the newspaper," said Mr. Vargas. "The ad could go on radio or TV, too."

The children laughed. They knew Mr. Vargas was joking. "That costs a lot of money," said Tom.

"Yes," Mr. Vargas said. "I know. I buy radio ads for my store. It's a good way of **communicating.**"

"What's communicating?" said Julie.

"Well, it's any way of sending a message," said Mr. Vargas. "Newspapers, radio, television, and magazines are some ways to let people know what's going on."

"So are all these signs," said Tom.

"That's right," said another man. "And one
of these signs told me who owns this cat."
He opened a box.

The children yelled with joy. "Toby!"

Lesson 1 Review

1. Why did the children put up a message?
2. What are some ways of communicating?
3. How would you let people know if you lost a
   pet?

Special People

Arielle Javitch

Arielle Javitch is a third grader in New York City. Arielle had an idea she wanted to communicate. She wrote a book called *Kitten Country*. In her book, some kittens get a job in the movies. Arielle wrote that kittens and children can learn when someone tells them what to do, but everyone learns best by doing.

Lesson 2

Why People Work

The Millers have a large family. They have many needs and wants. A **need** is something like food, clothes, or a house. It is anything we must have to live.

A **want** is something we would like to have but don't need. Family members earn money to provide for family needs and wants. Julie's grandmother earns money by typing. Julie's grandfather is a carpenter. Other people pay him to make the things they need.

Julie's mother works in an office. She runs a word processor. Julie's father and brother, Tom, earn money by selling the apples they grow on the Millers' farm. Tom helps after school. The Millers sometimes pay other people to help gather the apples.

Julie earns money by helping with jobs at home. Sometimes she takes care of her baby brother, Jesse. She would like a new bike. A new bike is not one of her needs but one of her wants.

Lesson 2 Review

1. What are some needs?
2. What are some wants?
3. How do people get what they need or want?
4. What other needs do people have that are different from Tom and Julie's?

Lesson 3

Apples to Market

Ron and Sue come to visit. They are
Tom and Julie's cousins. They live in a city.
It will be exciting for them to stay on a farm
for a while. On the ride home, Dad said, "Soon
you will see our **products.**"

"I thought products were made in factories," Sue said.

"That's true, too," said Dad. "Products are things people make or grow."

When they got to the farm, Dad sorted apples. "What happens next?" asked Ron.

This is how Mr. Miller explained what happens to his apples after he sells them to a company.

1. An apple grader sorts the apples by size.

2. Another machine packs the apples in boxes.

3. They are put in refrigerated trucks.

4. The trucks take the apples to stores.

5. The storekeeper sells them.

6. Somebody enjoys a fresh red apple.

"So that's how people get our apples," said Dad.

"And how we get money," added Tom.

Lesson 3 Review

1. What is a product?
2. Tell what happens in each step of the chart on page 50.
3. What are some of the products that are made or grown near your neighborhood?

Special Feature
Technology: Television

1. A script writer plans the story.

2. Then, an editor reads the script and makes it better.

3. Next, actresses and actors act out the story.

4. Or an artist draws the pictures on film.

5. Then, a cameraperson takes pictures with a camera.

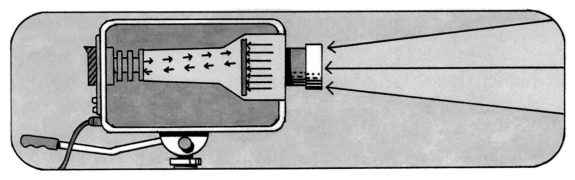

6. The camera changes the picture into electrical signals.

7. The signals are broadcast from a tall tower or with the help of a satellite.

8. Your television set changes the electrical signals back into pictures and sound.

Lesson 4

Neighborhood Helpers

The winters are cold where the Millers live. Houses need heat. The man in the picture is selling heating oil to the Millers. Bringing oil to a house is a **service**. A service is something people do for other people.

Electricity is the power that makes light bulbs bright. This woman checks the meter on the Millers' house. She sees how much electricity the family used. Then they get a bill for it. Providing electricity for homes is a service.

The post office and telephone company also provide services. This mail carrier from the U.S. Postal Service is bringing the Millers' mail. If the Millers' telephone breaks, the telephone company will send someone to fix it. Families need services to make life easier.

Many people bring services to your house. They earn money by helping people. Why might the people on this page come to your house?

Lesson 4 Review

1. What services did the Millers need?
2. What services do homes in your neighborhood need?
3. How do service workers earn money?

Skills for Thinking

Needs and Wants

You know that needs are things you must have. Wants are things you would like to have, but don't need. Look at the pictures.

1. Which pictures show needs?
2. Which pictures show wants?

Products and Services

Look at the pictures.

Make a chart.

1. In one row, list the jobs
where people are
making or growing products.

2. In another row, list the service jobs.

Unit 2 Review

Summary

- People need food, clothing, homes, and services.
- They work to earn money.
- They use money to pay for many things they need and want.

The Big Question

How do people get what they need?

Using Your New Words

Copy the sentences. Fill in the blanks.

service   electricity   need   product

1. Food and clothing are things people ____.

2. The food farmers grow is a ____.

3. Bringing oil to homes is a ____.

4. The money people earn pays for the ____ that lights their homes.

Test

Testing Skills

1. Look at the picture on page 60.
What products is the person buying?
What job is the worker doing?

2. Make a class bulletin board. Write messages
about school events and other news for it.

3. Interview some grown-ups. Ask them about
their jobs. Find out the different things
they do at work.

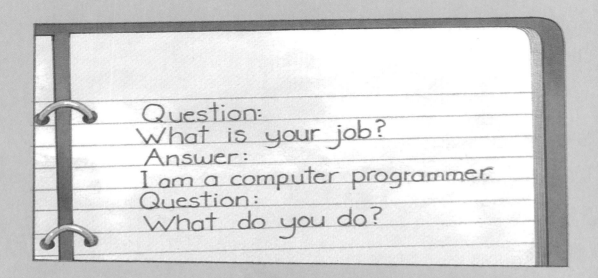

Question:
What is your job?
Answer:
I am a computer programmer.
Question:
What do you do?

Unit 3 Neighborhood Services

What is happening in the picture? How does this woman serve the people in the neighborhood? Who do you think pays for these services?

Words You Will Use

goods   library

tax money   transportation

The Big Question

How does a neighborhood serve its people?

Skills in This Unit

Making Inferences

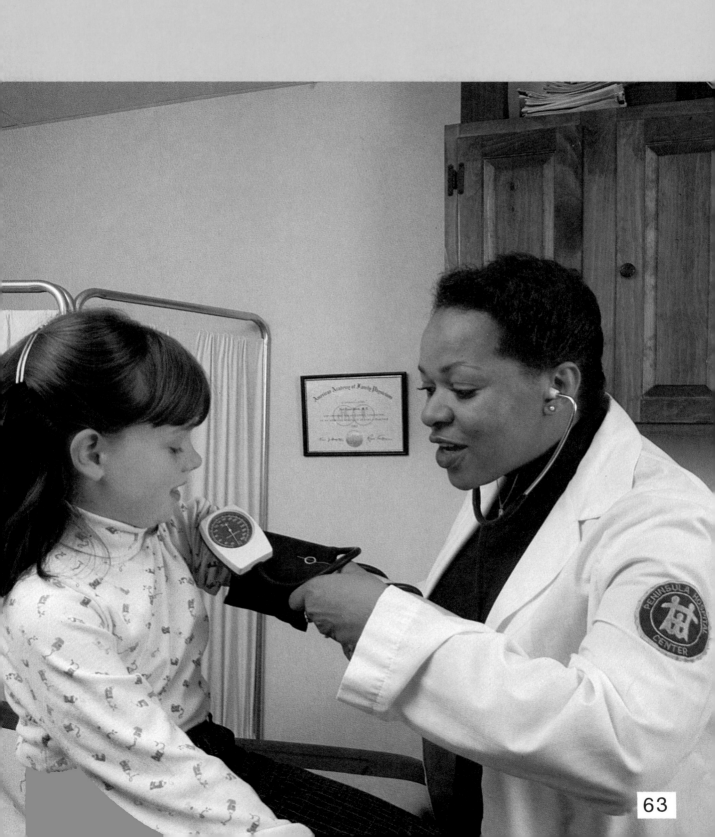

Grandma Goes Out

"Every Tuesday night you go out, Grandma," said Carla. "But nobody knows where you go."

Grandma laughed. "It's no big secret," she said. "Would you and Miguel like to come with me tonight?"

"Sure!" cried Miguel. "It sounds like fun!"

"Why are all these people here?" asked Carla.

"They come for many reasons," said Grandma. "Some are here to have fun. Others come to learn things."

"What do you come for?" asked Miguel.

"I come to learn and have fun," said Grandma. "Come on. You'll see."

"This is my teacher, Miss Rush," said
Grandma.

"You have a teacher?" said Miguel. "What
does she teach you?"

"I learn to draw and paint," said Grandma.

"You're an artist!" cried Carla.

"She's very good," said Miss Rush.

The neighborhood center is open to everyone. It is a meeting place for neighbors.

Lesson 1 Review

1. Why do people come to the neighborhood center?
2. How does Grandma have fun as she learns?
3. Do you have a neighborhood meeting place? How is it like Grandma's?

Special Feature

Citizenship: A Wonderful Sale

The neighborhood center needed money. It costs a lot to keep it running. The neighborhood decided to have a sale. People brought old clothes, books, and toys. They baked treats. Some people sewed or knitted clothes.

The people were selling **goods.** Goods are products that people make for sale. Some people make goods at their jobs. All these neighbors made goods to help the center.

They were successful. A lot of people came to the sale. The neighborhood celebrated.

Who Pays for It?

Miguel and Carla love going to the **library.** Carla looks around at the many books and chairs and tables.

"Who pays for all these books?" Carla asked.

Mother smiled. "We pay for them," she said.

Miguel was surprised. "We couldn't pay for the whole library! We aren't rich!" he said.

"We only pay a little of the cost," Mother explained. "Everyone who lives in town helps pay."

"When your father and I are paid at work, we pay a part of the money to the city," said Mother. "That money is **tax money.** Our tax money pays for neighborhood services like the library."

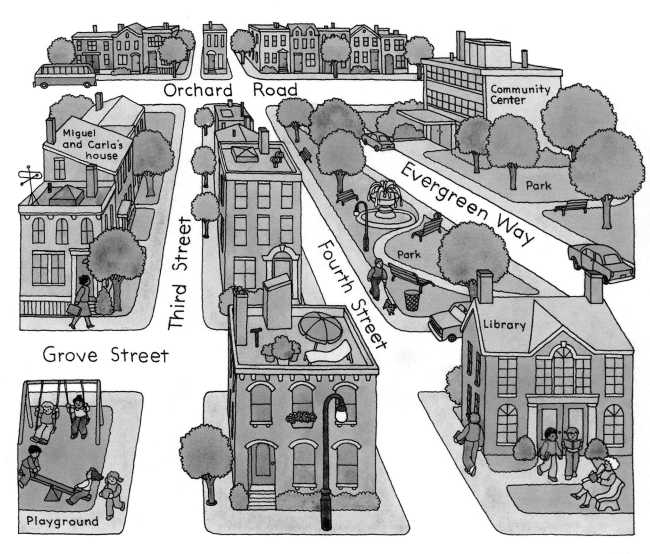

"The library is one neighborhood service and this is another," Mother said. She pointed to the garbage truck. Then Mother explained, "Stores and businesses also pay taxes. They help, too. Everyone pays, and everyone gets the services."

"Mom," called Miguel. "I'll bet tax money will pay to fix this!"

Lesson 2 Review

1. How are neighborhood services paid for?
2. What is tax money?
3. What services are in your neighborhood?

Lesson 3

The Best Way to Travel

What if apples from the Millers' farm were sent to the city on a dump truck? Would you want to eat those apples?

Transportation is any way of moving people or things around. Choosing the right kind of transportation is important.

The Millers' apples are really
shipped in trucks that keep the apples
cool and fresh.

Other products have special transportation
too. Bread trucks have trays so the
bread won't get crushed. Milk is sent in
tank trucks that keep liquids cool.

People use transportation, too. Here is a
street near Tom and Julie's home. What kinds
of transportation can you see? Which
would you use for going a long way?

Here is a street where Miguel and Carla live. What kinds of transportation would you find only in a city? What kinds might you find anywhere?

Lesson 3 Review

1. What kinds of transportation carry people? What kinds carry goods? What kinds carry both people and goods?
2. What kinds of transportation does your community have?

Skills for Thinking

Finding What You Want

When you want something, you have to know where to get it. How can you tell?
Look at the pictures.

Where would you go to find each of these?

Miguel and Carla are looking for these things.

1. Where will they find the first thing?
2. Where will they find the second thing?
3. Where should they go last?

Unit 3 Review

Summary

- Every neighborhood has services.
- Many services are paid for by tax money.
- Goods and people are moved by many kinds of transportation.

The Big Question

How does a neighborhood serve its people?

Using Your New Words

library   transportation   tax money   goods

Match one of your new words to the words below.

books   apples   community services   bus

  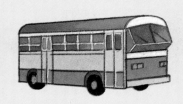 

Testing Skills

1. Look at the picture. Where do you think the truck is going? What service do the people in the truck provide to the neighborhood?

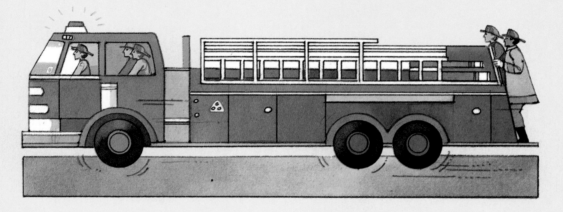

2. How many different ways have you traveled? Draw a picture of each way. Put the pictures on the class bulletin board.

Unit 4 Neighborhoods Have Rules

What are the signs for?
How are these children leaders?

Words You Will Use

rule   safety   leader
skill   volunteer

The Big Question

How do rules help neighborhoods
work?

Skills in This Unit

Sequencing

Playing by the Rules

"You can't throw from there!" said Donna.

"Yes, I can," said Jerry. "I can throw from anywhere I want to."

"That's not fair," cried Donna.

"It is so fair," Jerry said.

"Then I can throw from here," Donna said.
She stood right next to the post.
"No, you can't!" Jerry said.
"Why not?" asked Donna.
"That's not fair," said Jerry.
"Then what is fair?" Donna asked.

"You need a **rule**," Nina said. "Rules help make the game fair."

"What rule do we need?" asked Donna.

"Maybe you should both agree to throw from here," Nina said.

"All right," said Jerry. "We'll try it."

"I'm starting to like this game!" yelled Donna.

"It's more fun to play by the rules," Jerry said. "Rules help make things fair for everyone."

"May I play, too?" asked Nina.

Lesson 1 Review

1. Why did Jerry and Donna disagree?
2. What rule did they need?
3. Who makes rules?
4. What can happen when games don't have rules?

Lesson 2

We Know Rules

Rules help make games fair.

There are other reasons for rules. Rules help keep us safe. Rules help keep order.

Look at this picture. Why do these people need rules? What rules are needed?

This neighborhood has a pool. Everyone can use it. Neighbors can have a good time.

What rules does the pool have? Tell why each rule is needed.

These are **safety** rules. Who helps people obey the rules? How do they help?

What other safety rules do you know?

NO

- DIVING FROM SIDE OF POOL
- PETS IN POOL AREA
- RUNNING
- EVERYONE MUST SHOWER BEFORE ENTERING POOL

THE MANAGEMENT

Some rules can help to make a neighborhood a good place to live.

What rule has been broken in this park? Is it a fair rule? Should everyone follow this rule?

Are there signs in your neighborhood? What rules do they tell you about? What can happen when a rule is broken?

Obeying rules is important. Rules help everyone.

You know many rules. Tell what rules these children are obeying. How do the rules help?

Lesson 2 Review

1. How do rules help keep order?
2. How do rules help keep us safe?
3. What would a town be like if it had no rules?

Lesson 3

Choosing Leaders

Leaders are people who lead the way. They get things done by rules.

We choose different leaders for different reasons. Some leaders are chosen because they are the best at something. People who are good at something have a **skill.**

People can share their skills with others.
Who is the leader in this picture?
What skill does this leader have?

Leaders help people to work together.
They give each person a job to do. They see
that the job is done well. They set a good
example.

It takes hard work to be a good leader.
It can be fun, too. Every neighborhood
needs leaders.

Each of us has different skills.
We can all be leaders. How is this boy
being a leader?

Lesson 3 Review

1. What makes a good leader?
2. Look at the picture on page 93.
   Why do you think the girl is a leader?
3. Name another kind of leader.
4. Why do people need leaders?

Special Feature

Citizenship: Neighbors Help

Many people earn pay for doing jobs.
Volunteers are people who do jobs without pay.

Volunteers help neighborhoods in many ways. How do these volunteers help? Do you know other ways to help?

Lesson 4

Solving Neighborhood Problems

The children of Greene Street weren't happy about where they played.

"This place isn't fun anymore," said Hector.

"But it is the only place to play," said Paul.

"Maybe we could fix it up," said Shelly.

"How could we do that?" said Hector. "It would take money and more people."

"I think I know who can help," said Shelly.

"My dad knows Mr. Hughes," Shelly said. "He is a neighborhood leader."

The children went to see Mr. Hughes.

"We think the lot would make a great park for the neighborhood," said Hector.

"That's a good idea," Mr. Hughes said. "The lot belongs to the city. Maybe we can do something. Can you come to a meeting to tell people your idea?"

"Sure we can," said Shelly.

"If we all worked together, we could make
a new park for everyone to enjoy," said Shelly.

"Who will help?" asked Mr. Hughes.

"I know where we can buy plants," said
one man.

"I have a bench for people to sit on,"
said a woman.

"I could paint a sign for the park," said
another man.

"Tomorrow the park will open," said Paul.

"It was easy to do the job with so much help," Shelly smiled.

"This park really belongs to the neighborhood," said Hector.

Lesson 4 Review

1. How did the lot get changed into a park? Who had the idea? Who helped?
2. Tell about a neighborhood problem you would like to help solve.

Skills for Thinking

What Are the Rules?

Here is a game Native Americans played. Find out how to play.

Players stand in a circle. One player kicks the ball to another.

The ball must stay in the air. Players can only use their feet. If a player lets the ball drop, he or she is out.

Now think about this.
1. If you caught the ball, would you win?
2. How does this game end?
3. Why are rules important in this game?

These rules tell about a game. The rules are out of order. Guess what the game is.

Everyone pulls.
A team that crosses the line loses.
There are two teams.
A line is drawn between the teams.
Each team holds one end of a rope.

1. Which rule should go first?
2. Which rule should go last?
3. Which rules tell what the teams do?

Unit 4 Review

Summary

- Rules help keep order.
- Rules keep people safe.
- Rules make things fair for everyone.
- Leaders help people work together.

The Big Question

How do rules help neighborhoods work?

Using Your New Words

rule   safety   volunteer

leader   skill

Write the words on paper.

For each word, give an example.

Test

Testing Skills

1. Signs show us many rules. Some signs have no words. Look at these signs. What rules do they give?

2. You have rules in your classroom. Make a sign to show one rule.

No talking in class.

3. Name some leaders. Use the pictures to help.

Unit 5 Neighborhoods Change

Sometimes a neighborhood needs a change. What is happening here? People can make a difference. Neighbors can work together to make a better life.

Words You Will Use

factory	renew	fuel
energy	present	future

The Big Question

How do neighborhoods change?

Skills in This Unit

Drawing Conclusions

Lesson 1

Neighborhoods of the Past

Rachel and Henry were excited. This was the day of the "logrolling." A new family had come. Everyone from miles around was coming to help them build a house.

Rachel and Henry lived over 200 years ago. Neighborhoods were different then. There weren't so many people. People didn't have many machines to help them, but people helped each other a lot. That made things easier for everybody.

Suppose you and your parents had to build a house all by yourselves. It would take a long time. That was why people had logrollings. When neighbors worked together, the house could be built quickly. Some people cut down the trees. Others rolled the logs to the place where the house was being built. Neighbors helped to build schools and churches by working together, too.

Lesson 1 Review

1. Why did people have logrollings long ago?

2. How do neighbors help each other today?

Lesson 2

A Neighborhood Story

Your neighborhood was not always as it is now. Long ago, it may have been a forest or farmland.

The neighborhood in the picture began because of a bicycle **factory.** A factory is a place where people make products, such as bicycles. People went to the area to work in the factory. Stores that sold food and clothes opened. People built homes nearby. They also built a school for their children.

Over the years, this neighborhood changed. Leaders worked together to take care of neighborhood needs. Water and sewer pipes were put underground. Poles for electric and telephone wires were put up. Streets and sidewalks were built. What other things did the leaders need to do?

People planted trees and gardens. They enjoyed sharing parks and a library. They liked their neighborhood.

After a long time, things changed. The bicycle company closed the factory. There were few jobs. People moved away. Houses were not cared for. Windows were broken and roofs leaked.

Stores closed because there were not enough people to buy things. The neighborhood became quiet and sad.

When neighbors move away, there are fewer people to take care of things. What happens then?

Then the town's leaders got a computer company to start a factory there. Soon there were more jobs in the neighborhood. People bought houses and fixed them up. New stores opened. The neighborhood had new growth and new hope.

Lesson 2 Review

1. What are some needs of a neighborhood?
2. How can a neigborhood become run-down?
3. Tell some ways that people can get a run-down neighborhood to grow again.

Lesson 3

Neighborhoods Are Renewed

Mr. Barnes got a job in the new computer factory. The family decided to move from their old neighborhood to be near the factory.

"Are we going to live here?" said Mark. "It's not a very pretty house."

"It can change," Mr. Barnes said. "We can buy the house at a low price."

"But it's all run-down," said Tania.

"We'll work to fix it up," Mrs. Barnes said.

The children whistled. "That's a big job."

"This room looks a lot bigger now," said
Tania. "A coat of paint really helped. I like it
better than my old bedroom."

"Old houses can be good places to live,"
Mrs. Barnes said.

"Look outside," Mark said. "Some city workers
are planting trees."

"And another family moved in next door,"
Tania said. "This is going to be a great
neighborhood."

The neighborhood is being **renewed.**
To renew is to make things look new again.
Many old neighborhoods are being renewed
today. People are helping to build new
neighborhoods in old places.

Lesson 3 Review

1. How did the Barneses help renew their
   neighborhood?
2. Why did people want to move into old
   houses?

Special People

James R. Doman, Jr.

James Doman is an architect. Architects decide how to build buildings. They plan new neighborhoods. They also plan how to fix up old neighborhoods. In one neighborhood many homes became run-down. The people moved away. Mr. Doman made plans and hired workers to fix the buildings. Now people are living in the neighborhood again. Mr. Doman is proud of his work. The picture shows a house he fixed up.

Special Feature

Technology: Solar Homes

Many people use **fuels** such as coal, oil, or gas to heat their homes. These fuels have to be burned to make heat and **energy.** Energy is the power that makes machines run. When coal, oil, and gas burn, they make fire and smoke. They also cost more now than they did in the past.

Scientists are finding cheaper and cleaner ways to get energy. One way is to use the energy of the sun, solar energy.

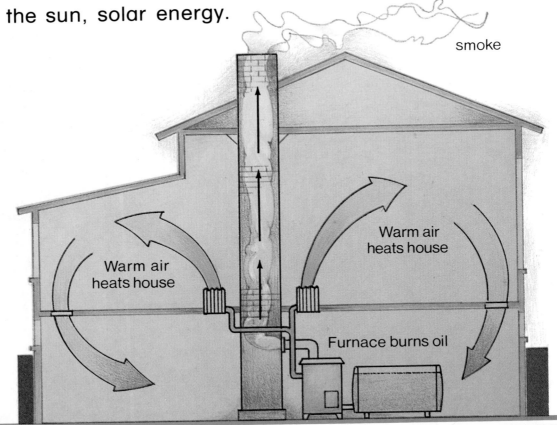

smoke

Warm air heats house

Warm air heats house

Furnace burns oil

The house in the picture uses solar energy. The glass on the roof catches the sun's rays. The energy from the sun's rays can be stored and used to heat water. The heated water can then be used for washing or it can be sent through pipes to heat the whole house. People don't have to pay for the sun's rays. Why else might people wish to use solar energy instead of gas, oil, or coal?

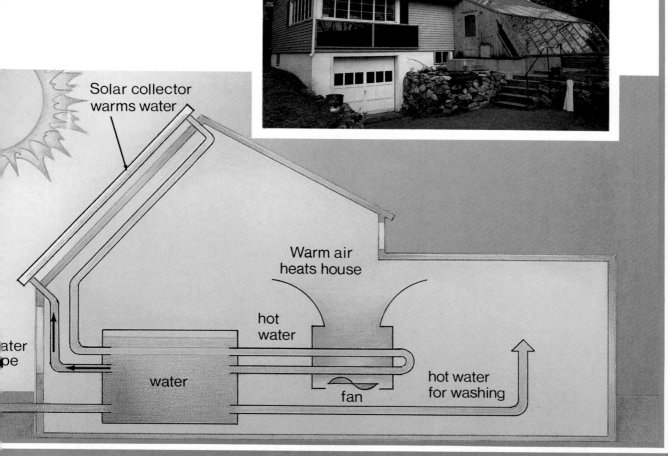

Solar collector warms water

Warm air heats house

hot water

water

fan

hot water for washing

ater pe

Lesson 4

Neighborhoods of Tomorrow

Remember Rachel's and Henry's neighborhood of the past. Think about your own neighborhood today, in the **present.** What do you think neighborhoods of the **future** will be like? The future is tomorrow and all the days after that. You will live all the rest of your life in the future. Look at the picture of EPCOT Center at Walt Disney World in Florida. Do you think your neighborhood will someday be like EPCOT Center?

The Earth will probably be more crowded in the future. People may use the bottom of the ocean for farming. Robots may do many of the jobs on these farms. In the future, there may be factories in space. Who do you think might work in those factories?

Imagine travel in the future. How will children get to school? Where will people go for vacations?

Telephones and television are two ways to communicate today. There are even telephones for people who do not hear well. Today, we can talk to some machines and tell them what to do. Some machines talk to us. For example, a car computer can remind us to fasten the seatbelt. What new ways of communicating can you imagine in the future?

Classrooms, too, will probably be very different in the future. Where do you think children of the future will go to learn? What will the place look like? What will the teachers do? How might computers and robots help?

Lesson 4 Review

1. How might transportation in the future be different from transportation today?
2. How might communication be different?
3. What might schools be like in the future?

Skills for Thinking

Clues to the Past

The pictures on the next page show the same neighborhood at four different times.

1. Which picture shows the neighborhood when it first started?
2. Which shows how people renewed the neighborhood?
3. Which picture shows the neighborhood at its worst?

Now think about this.

4. Pretend that you are one of the houses in this neighborhood. Write about what happened to you in these pictures.
5. What will this neighborhood look like in the future? Draw a picture showing what it will look like.

Summary

- Neighborhoods are planned to meet people's needs.
- Neighborhoods grow and change.
- Neighborhoods can be renewed.
- Neighborhoods of the future will be different.

The Big Question

How do neighborhoods change?

Using Your New Words

Use each of these words in a sentence.

renew	energy	present
future	fuel	factory

Test

Testing Skills

1. Make a list of the things your neighborhood needs. Tell how people could provide for those needs.
2. What are some of the ways neighbors helped each other in the past? How can you help your neighbors in the present? In the future?
3. Would you rather live in a neighborhood of the past or in a neighborhood of the future? Why?

Unit 6 Neighborhoods All Over

The Earth is a big place with many people in it. People everywhere have the same needs. You may be surprised at the different ways people meet those needs.

Words You Will Use

volcano   plain   island
harbor   lava   subway

The Big Question

How are neighborhoods in other countries different from yours?

Skills in This Unit

Making Inferences

Lesson 1

Dear Pen Pal

Paco

Mia

Chumbhit

Alberto

Idella

Paco and Mia joined a pen pal club. A pen pal is a friend you write to in another country.

The pen pal club gave three addresses to Paco and Mia. They wrote letters to three boys and girls in other countries.

Here is what Paco and Mia wrote.

Dear Chumphit (CHOOM*pit),

We live in Los Angeles, California, in the United States. Los Angeles is a large city with many neighborhoods. Our neighborhood is near the ocean. We like to go there and play on the beach.

Los Angeles has many streets. You need a car to get to most places. We have a shopping center near our home. We can buy almost everything we need there.

Hollywood is one of Los Angeles's
neighborhoods. Many movies are made near here.
If you came to visit, you might see people making
a movie. Our mother works at a movie studio.

We would like to know about your city.
Will you tell us about it in your letter?

Your pen pals,

Paco and Mia

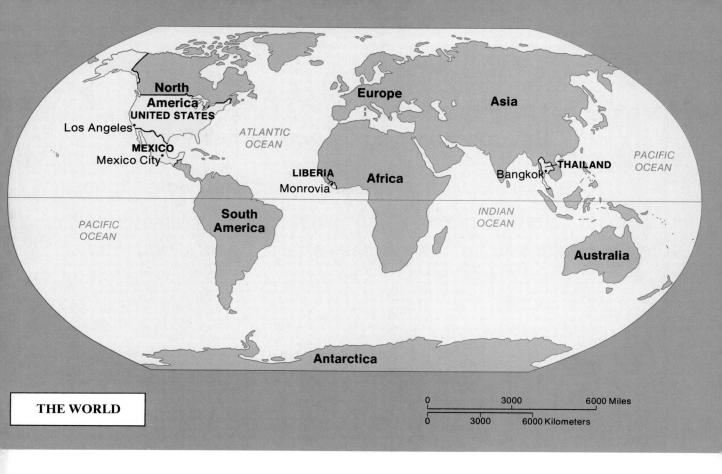

North America
UNITED STATES
Los Angeles
MEXICO
Mexico City

ATLANTIC OCEAN

Europe

Asia

PACIFIC OCEAN

LIBERIA
Monrovia

Africa

Bangkok **THAILAND**

South America

INDIAN OCEAN

PACIFIC OCEAN

Australia

Antarctica

THE WORLD

0   3000   6000 Miles

0   3000   6000 Kilometers

This map of the world shows the places where Paco's and Mia's pen pals live.

Lesson 1 Review

1. What kind of transportation do Paco and Mia say you need in Los Angeles?
2. Where does Paco's and Mia's family buy the things it needs?
3. How is Paco's and Mia's city like yours? How is it different?

Special Feature

Environment: Land and Water Forms

There are many kinds of land and water forms in different parts of the world. Here are some you could find in the places where Paco's and Mia's pen pals live.

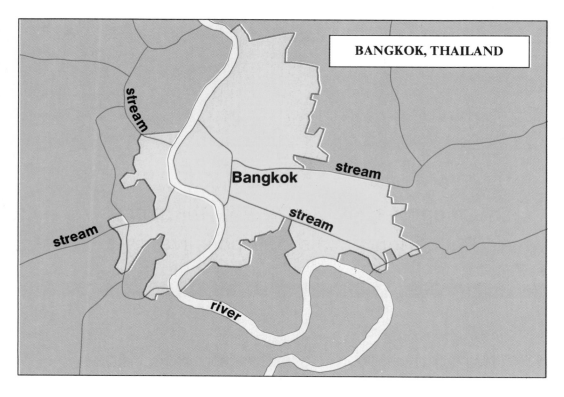

A river runs through Bangkok, Thailand. A river can be important to a city. Boats often carry goods to and from the city. In Bangkok, small streams flow into this river.

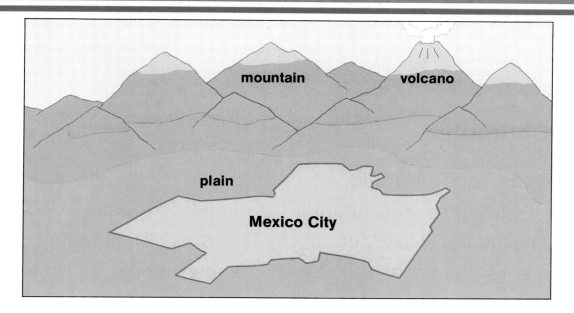

Mountains and volcanoes surround Mexico City, Mexico. A mountain is higher than a hill. A **volcano** is a mountain formed from melted rock and ash. The city is on flat land called a **plain.**

Part of Monrovia, Liberia is on an **island.** An island is a small piece of land with water all around it. Monrovia has a good **harbor.** A harbor is protected water where ships can load and unload safely.

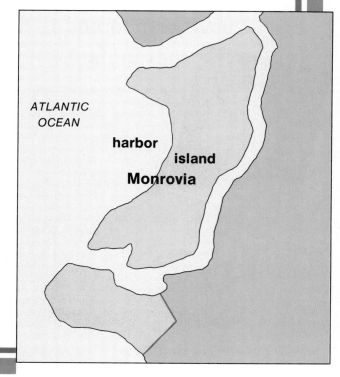

Lesson 2

Chumbhit

Dear Paco and Mia,

My name is Chumbhit. Bangkok is my city. The name of my country is Thailand. Thailand means "Land of the Free." I know people call the United States that, too. People everywhere must like to be free.

I'd like to tell you some things about my city. Bangkok is on the Chao Phraya River (*chow**PRAY*ah). I live along the river. There are also little streams flowing through my neighborhood. Some people use boats to get around.

We buy our food from people who have their shops on small boats. This morning I went down our front steps to a boat shop and bought a fried egg.

In the mornings the little streams are filled with boats. People are selling fruit, cakes, and flowers. I think they must be as crowded as Los Angeles's streets. Sometimes we ride the bus to a big market to buy our food.

On the other side of the river, the city
is different. Many new offices and apartments
have been built. The streets there are
probably more like yours. They are filled
with people and cars. This part of the city
is very busy with people going to and from
their jobs.

Bangkok has many old buildings, too. I would like you to see the Grand Palace. Our king lives there. I think you would like the old temples with golden roofs.

Yours truly,

Chumbhit

Lesson 2 Review

1. Where does Chumbhit's family buy things it needs?

2. What kind of transportation do some people in Chumbhit's neighborhood use?

3. How is Bangkok's river neighborhood different from Paco and Mia's neighborhood in Los Angeles?

4. How are the two neighborhoods alike?

Lesson 3

Alberto

Dear Paco and Mia,

My name is Alberto. I live in Mexico City, Mexico. Mexico City is even larger than Los Angeles. It is one of the biggest cities in the world. More than 9 million people live here.

I am lucky. I live in Pedregal (ped*ra*GALL), which is a nice neighborhood. Our home is new and large. Other neighborhoods in Mexico City are older and more crowded. Many, many people move here to find jobs.

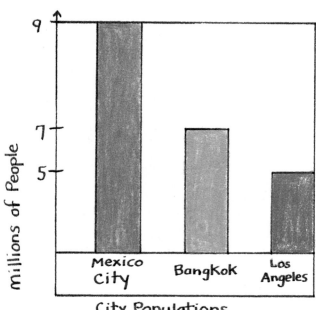

City Populations

The ground under our house is hard and black. It is **lava.** Lava is hot melted rock that shoots out of volcanoes. It flows down the mountainside. Then it cools and hardens. There are volcanoes all around the city. Don't worry. Lava has not bubbled up and out of them in a long time.

A good way to travel in our city is by **subway,** a train that runs underground. Our subway is new and clean. The stations have beautiful paintings on the walls.

We have a big park in our neighborhood.
It's fun to go there and play. There are
mariachi (mah*ree*AH*chee) bands. The bands
play any song you ask for. And you can buy
all kinds of food. I like mole poblano
(MOH*lay*poh*BLAH*no). That is turkey with
chili and chocolate. I think you'd like it!

Mexico City is an old city. The first people to live here were the Aztecs. Here is a picture of the Plaza of the Three Cultures. You can see part of the old Aztec city, a Spanish church, and modern buildings.

Sincerely yours,

Alberto

Lesson 3 Review

1. How is a Mexico City neighborhood different from a neighborhood in Los Angeles?
2. What is one way to travel from one neighborhood to another in Mexico City?
3. How are Bangkok, Mexico City, and Los Angeles alike?

Lesson 4

Idella

Dear Paco and Mia,

My name is Idella. I live in Monrovia, Liberia. Monrovia is named after a president of the United States, James Monroe. The city was begun by black people from the United States. Our two countries have been friendly for a long time.

Monrovia is on the ocean. It is on the west coast of Africa. I live in the part of the city called Bushrod Island. Some of the city is on the mainland. Mainland means a large piece of land, not a small island.

The people in my neighborhood belong to a group called the Kru. There are many different groups in Liberia. They are like big families. Each group has its own language, but most people also speak English. That makes it easier to talk to people from other groups.

People in my family are weavers. Weavers make cloth. Like many families, we have our shop inside our house. Children learn the work that their parents do. We help earn money for our family.

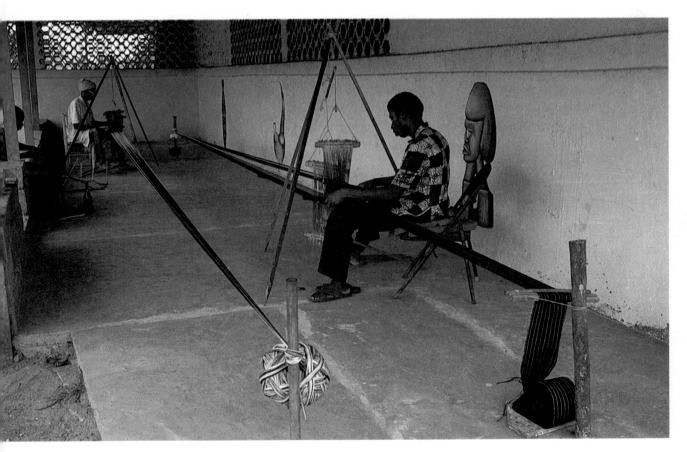

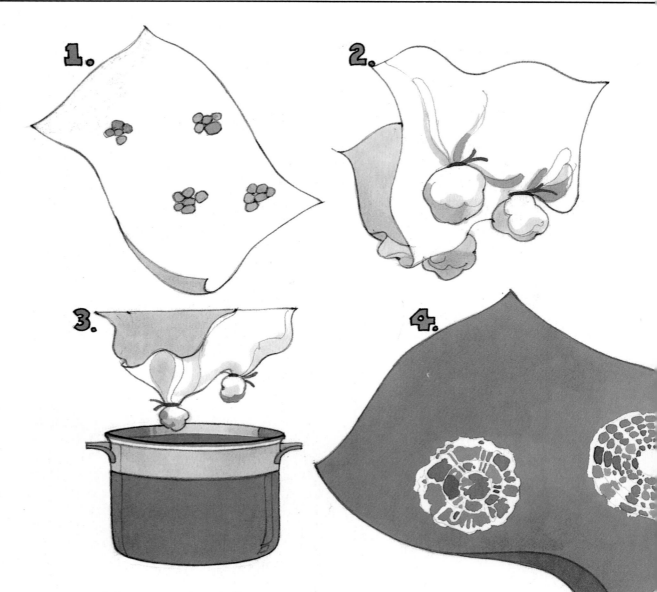

After we weave cloth, we dye, or color it.
Our mother showed us how to tie-dye cloth to
make it beautiful. We put small stones inside
the cloth. Then we tie knots around them.
Then we put the cloth in a big pot of dye.
When we untie the knots, there is a beautiful
pattern. People want to buy our cloth
because we dye it so well.

There are so many things to do and see in Monrovia. If you were here, we could go to the market on a Saturday. That is when people bring food from their farms to sell. We would probably take a taxi to the market. You pay a taxi driver to take you to places you want to go. Most people use taxis to get around in Monrovia.

On holidays, we could go to the country to see the stilt dancers. These people dance on stilts 10 feet high. We could also listen to storytellers. My favorite stories are about Anansi, the spider who tricks people.

We can also go to the harbor. There are always ships there. All along the ocean shore are lovely white sandy beaches. You can swim or catch your own fish. Come visit soon!

Your pen pal,

Idella

Lesson 4 Review

1. How does Idella help her family?

2. Where does Idella's family buy food?

3. How is Monrovia like the other cities where Paco and Mia have pen pals? How is it different?

Special People

Kimani Rogers

When Kimani Rogers was 8 years old, he and his family visited Africa. While they were in Njala (en*JAH*lah), Sierra Leone (see*AIR*ah*lee*OHN), Kimani met Amy and Brian Davis. The children became friends. They played soccer, or football, Kimani's favorite sport. When Kimani got home, he wrote a letter to Amy and Brian. They wrote back and sent some photographs, too. Now the children have become regular pen pals.

Skills for Thinking

The Way People Live

Climate often affects the way people live. Remember, climate is the kind of weather in a place over a long time.

Thailand has a long rainy season. When it rains, the water in the streams and rivers rises. What is special about the houses in the picture? Why do you think they are built this way?

These African houses are made of palm leaves and straw. Are they better for a warm climate or a cold climate?

Climate can also affect the way that people have fun. These children in the country of Sweden enjoy ice-skating. How does climate affect what they are doing? How does it affect what they wear?

Los Angeles is warm much of the year. How does that climate affect what these children are doing for fun? What other ways do you think the children of Los Angeles can enjoy themselves?

Unit 6 Review

Summary

- People have the same needs in all neighborhoods.
- In different places, people meet their needs in different ways.
- Location and climate cause differences in neighborhoods around the world.

The Big Question

How are neighborhoods in other countries different from yours?

Using Your New Words

Write a sentence using each of these words.

harbor   island   volcano

plain   lava   subway

Test

Testing Skills

	Your Community	Los Angeles	Bangkok	Mexico City	Monrovia
Land		beaches, near ocean		plain with mountains around	
Homes			some on stilts, some apartments		
Shopping				marketplace	
Transportation					taxis
Having Fun		Swimming			

Copy the chart. Fill in the missing parts.

- How are homes different in each city?
- How is transportation different in each place?
- How is having fun the same?
- Look at your completed chart. Tell what you think it would be like to live in each city.

Glossary

This glossary has many words used in *America's Neighborhoods.* Each word is followed by its meaning and a number. The number tells you the unit where you can find the word.

architect A person who decides how and where to build buildings. (5)

city A place where many people live and work together. (6)

climate The kind of weather in a place over a long time. (6)

communicating Any way of sending a message. (2)

dye To color things, like clothes. (6)

Earth The place, or planet, where we live. (6)

electricity A form of power that makes light and heat. (2)

energy Power that makes things work. (5)

factory A place where people make products. (5)

fuel Anything that can be burned to produce heat and energy. Oil, wood, and coal are fuels. (5)

future Tomorrow and all the days after that; time to come. (5)

globe A ball with a map of Earth on it.

goods Products that people make for sale. Oranges and bicycles are goods. (3)

harbor A protected area of water where ships can load and unload safely. (6)

island A small piece of land with water all around it. (6)

lava Hot melted rock that shoots out of volcanos. (6)

leader A person who leads the way and helps others to work together. (4)

library A building where books, magazines, films and records are kept and borrowed. (3)

mainland A large piece of land, not a small island. (6)

154

map A flat drawing of a place that shows where things are. (1)

mountain Raised land that is higher than a hill. (6)

need Anything people must have to live, like food or clothes. (2)

neighbor A person who lives in the house or apartment close to you. (1)

neighborhood A small part of a town or city where people live near one another. (1)

ocean A large body of salt water. (1)

past Yesterday and all the days before; time which has gone by. (1)

plain A flat area of land. (6)

present Today or now. (5)

products Things people make or grow. Apples and toys are products. (2)

renew To make things look new. (5)

river A large stream of water. (6)

rule Agreement of what is fair and safe to do. (4)

safety Freedom from harm and danger. (4)

service Useful work that people do to help. (2)

skill Ability to do something well. (4)

soccer A game where the players try to kick a ball without touching it with their hands. (6)

solar energy Power from the sun. (5)

state One of the fifty parts of the United States. (1)

subway A train that runs underground. (6)

taxi A car that people pay to ride in. (6)

tax money Money people and businesses pay to the government. Taxes pay for community goods and services. (3)

town A small place where people live and work together. (1)

transportation Any way of moving people or things from place to place. (3)

volcano A mountain formed from melted rock and ash. (6)

volunteer A person who does a job without pay. (4)

want Something a person would like to have but does not need. (2)

weavers People who make cloth. (6)

world Earth and all the people and things on it. (6)

Index

The words and numbers in this index show you the pages where you can find information about people, places, and things in *America's Neighborhoods*. Words followed by a star ★ are Words You Will Use.

Credits

Cover and Text Design
Sheaff Design, Inc.

Cover and Title Page
Steve Dunwell

Maps
John and Dick Sanderson

Illustrations
Bert Dodson: 10, 11, 13, 14, 17, 22, 23, 24, 25, 28, 29, 30, 31
Len Ebert: 32, 33, 34, 58, 59, 60, 61, 78, 79, 80, 81 top, 102, 103, 104, 105, 125, 126, 127, 146, 150, 151, 152, 154
James Barabas: 35, 81 bottom
John Killgrew: 50, 51, 52
Samantha Smith: 68, 69
Ethel Gold: 71, 74, 75, 76, 77

Jan Palmer: 88–89, 90, 98, 99, 100, 101
Shelly Freshman: 108, 109
Michael Adams: 110, 111, 112, 113, 114, 115, 116
Louis Pappas: 118, 119

Photography

James Foote: 15, 16, 18, 20
Michael Hardy: 37–42, 44–49, 53–56, 63
Laurie Leifer Helman: 43
Michal Heron: 58–61, 70, 73, 93, 95, 97, 130 top left, top center, 131 both insets
Robert Gray: 72, 84–87, 91 left, 149
Anthony Barboza: 117
Courtesy of S. Paleewong: 130
Alfred Butler: 130 bottom left, 140 inset

Photographs

Peter Arnold Inc.:
Jacques Jangoux: 148
Bruce Coleman:
Lee Foster: 57
Image Bank:
Joseph Brignolo: 139
John Bryson: 128–129, 132
Larry Dale Gordon: 26
Patti McConville: 138
Guido Alberto Rossi: 120
Charles Weckler: 136
Monkmeyer Press Photo:
Hugh Rogers: 21
Photo Researchers:
Robert deGast: 27
Victor Englebert: 143
Dana Hyde: 122
Michael Phillip Manheim: 92
Susan McCartney: 137
Pamela Johnson Meyer: 130 bottom right, 144

Larry Mulvehill: 57, 94
M.Seraillier: 121
Catherine Ursillo: 106–107
Bernard Pierre Wolfe: 144, 145, 147
Picture Cube:
James H. Simon: 119
Taurus:
Mark Mittleman: 82–83
Pam Hasegawa: 91
Eric Kroll: 19
Woodfin Camp & Associates, Inc.,
Craig Auress: 131
Nathan Bern: 8–9
Marc & Evelyn Bernheim: 141
Gerald Davis: 123
Michal Heron: 96
Stock Market:
Randy O'Rourke: 21
Vince Streano: 142

BCDEFGHIJ0898765
Printed in the United States of America